The Fabian Society

The Fabian Society has played a central role for
development of political ideas and public polic
the key challenges facing the UK and the rest ‹
changing society and global economy, the So‹
explore the political ideas and the policy reforms which ....
politics in the new century.

The Society is unique among think tanks in being a democratically-constituted
membership organisation. It is affiliated to the Labour Party but is editorially
and organisationally independent. Through its publications, seminars and
conferences, the Society provides an arena for open-minded public debate.

Fabian Society
11 Dartmouth Street
London SW1H 9BN
www.fabian-society.org.uk

Fabian ideas
Editor: Adrian Harvey
Design: Rory Fisher

First published December 2000

ISBN 0 7163 0598 4
ISSN 1469 0136

British Library Cataloguing in Publication data.
A catalogue record for this book is available from the British Library.

Printed by Bell & Bain Limited, Glasgow

Contents

About the author

Colin Crouch is Professor of Sociology at the European University Institute, Florence, and External Scientific member of the Max Planck Institute for Society Research, Cologne. He is chairman of the editorial board of the *Political Quarterly*, of which he was previously joint editor. He was Chairman of the Fabian Society in 1976. His recent books include *Industrial Relations and European State Traditions* (1993), *Are Skills the Answer?* (with David Finegold and Mari Sako, 1999), and *Social Change in Western Europe* (1999).

1 | Why Post-Democracy

M y theme is the poor health of democracy. Many will regard this as a strange pre-occupation at a time when democracy could be said to be enjoying a world-historical peak. But this peak relates to the minimal though admittedly absolutely vital criterion of democracy as the choice of governments in free elections based on universal adult suffrage. I want however to go beyond such minimalism and appraise our current democratic practices in the light of an admittedly ambitious maximal model.

Democracy thrives when there are major opportunities for the mass of ordinary people actively to participate, through discussion and autonomous organisations, in shaping the agenda of public life, and when these opportunities are being actively used by them. This is ambitious in expecting very large numbers of people to participate actively in serious political discussion and in framing the agenda, rather than be the passive respondents to opinion polls, and to be knowledgeably engaged in following political events and issues. This is an ideal model which can almost never be fully achieved, but like all impossible ideals it sets a marker. It is always valuable and intensely practical to consider where our conduct stands in relation to an ideal, since in that way we can try to improve. It is essential to take this approach to democracy rather than the more common one, which is to scale down definitions of the ideal so that they conform to what we easily achieve. That way lies complacency, self-congratulation, and an absence of concern to identify ways in which democracy is being weakened.

The issue becomes more intriguing when we confront the ambitious ideal, not with the simple minimal model of the existence of more or less free and fair elections, but with what I have in mind as post-democracy. Under this model, while elections certainly exist and can change governments, public electoral debate is a tightly controlled spectacle, managed by rival teams of professionals expert in the techniques of persuasion, and considering a small range of issues selected by those teams. The mass of citizens plays a passive, quiescent, even apathetic part, responding only to the signals given them. Behind this spectacle of the electoral game politics is really shaped in private by interaction between elected governments and elites which overwhelmingly represent business interests.

This model, like the maximal ideal, is also an exaggeration, but enough elements of it are recognisable in contemporary politics to make it worth while asking where our political life stands on a scale running between it and the maximal democratic model; and in particular to appraise in which direction it seems to be moving between them. It is my contention that we are increasingly moving towards the post-democratic pole.

If I am right about this, the factors which I shall identify as causing the movement also help explain something else, of particular concern to social democrats, Fabians and other egalitarians.[1] Under the conditions of post-democracy there is clearly little hope for an agenda of strong egalitarian policies for the redistribution of power and wealth, or for the restraint of powerful interests. If politics is becoming post-democratic in this sense, then on the political left we shall experience a transformation in the relationship between political parties and social causes as profound as that which took place at the start of the 20th century. This was when Beatrice Webb and others turned from the task of lobbying, as outsiders, politicians of the Conservative and Liberal Parties on behalf of radical causes to that of helping to found a Labour Party that would itself directly stand for those causes. A post-democratic transformation would take us back to where she started.

This does not mean coming full circle, because as well as moving in the opposite direction we are located at a different point in historical time and carry that inheritance with us. Rather, democracy has moved in a parabola. If you trace the outline of a parabola, your pen passes one of the co-ordinates twice: going in towards the centre of the parabola, and then again at a different point on the way out. This image will be important to much of what I have to say below about the complex characteristics of post-democracy.

Elsewhere I have written about 'The parabola of working-class politics' (in Gamble, A and Wright, T (eds.), *The New Social Democracy*, Oxford: Blackwell, 1999). I had in mind how, during the course of the 20th century, that class moved from being a weak, excluded, but increasingly numerous and strong force banging on the door of political life; through having its brief moment at the centre, in the period of formation of the welfare state, Keynesian demand management, and institutionalised industrial relations; to end as a numerically declining and increasingly disorganised grouping being expelled from that life as the achievements of the mid-century are booted out after it.

But I believe that the decline of the manual working class is only one, important, aspect of the parabolic experience of democracy itself. The two issues, the crisis of egalitarian politics and the trivialisation of democracy, are not necessarily the same. Egalitarians might say that they do not care how much manipulative spin a government uses, provided it divides society's wealth and power more evenly. A Conservative democrat will point out that improving the quality of political debate need not necessarily result in more redistributive policies. But at certain crucial points the two issues do intersect, and it is on this intersection that I intend to focus. My central contentions are that, while the forms of democracy remain fully in place—and today in some respects are actually strengthened—politics and government are increasingly slipping back into the control of privileged elites in the manner characteristic of pre-democratic times; and that one major consequence of this process is the growing impotence of egalitarian causes. This situation radically changes the assumptions about politics which Fabian egalitarians have been accustomed to make. Another implication is that to view the ills of democracy as just the fault of the mass media and the rise of spin-doctors is to miss some far more profound processes which are currently at work.

The democratic moment

Societies probably come closest to democracy in my maximal sense in the early years of achieving it or after great regime crises, when enthusiasm for it is widespread, many diverse groups and organisations of ordinary people share in the task of trying to frame a political agenda which will at last respond to their concerns; when the powerful interests which dominate undemocratic societies are wrong-footed and thrown on the defensive; and when the political system has not quite discovered how to manage and manipulate the new demands.

In most of western Europe and North America we had our democratic moment around the mid-point of the 20th century: slightly before the Second World War in North American and Scandinavia; soon after it for the rest of us. By then, not only had the final great movements of resistance against democracy—fascism and nazism—been defeated in a global war, but political change moved in tandem with a major economic development which made possible the realisation of many democratic goals. For the first time in the history of capitalism, the general health of the economy was seen as depending on the prosperity of the mass of wage-earning people. This was clearly expressed in the economic policies associated with Keynesianism, but also in the logic of the cycle of mass production and mass consumption embodied in so-called Fordist production methods. In those industrial societies which did not become communist, a certain social compromise was reached between capitalist business interests and working people. In exchange for the survival of the capitalist model and the general quietening of protest against the inequalities it produced, business interests learned to accept certain limitations on their capacity to use their power. And democratic political power concentrated at the level of the nation state was able to guarantee those limitations, as firms were largely subordinate to the authority of national states.

The high level of widespread political involvement of the early years, which was in any case partly a residue of the intensified public character of life during war itself, could not be sustained for many years. Elites soon learned how to manage and manipulate. People became disillusioned, bored or preoccupied with the business of everyday life. The growing complexity of issues after the major initial achievements of reform made it increasingly difficult to take up informed positions, to make intelligent comment, or even to know what 'side' one was on. Participation in political organisations declined almost everywhere, and eventually even the minimal act of voting was beset by apathy. Nevertheless the basic democratic imperatives of an economy dependent on the cycle of mass production and mass consumption sustained by public spending maintained the main policy impetus of the mid-century moment until the mid-1970s.

The oil crises of that decade tested to destruction the capacity

5

of the Keynesian system to manage inflation. The rise of the service economy reduced the role played by manual workers in sustaining the production/consumption cycle. By the late 1980s, the global deregulation of financial markets had shifted the emphasis of economic dynamism away from mass consumption and on to stock exchanges. The maximisation of shareholder value became the main indicator of economic success; debates about a wider stakeholder economy went very quiet. Everywhere the share in income taken by labour as opposed to capital, which had risen steadily for decades, began to decline again. The democratic economy had been tamed alongside the democratic polity.

Given the difficulty of sustaining anything approaching maximal democracy, declines from democratic moments must be accepted as inevitable, barring major new moments of crisis and change which permit a new re-engagement—or, more realistically in a society in which universal suffrage has been achieved, the emergence of new identities within the existing framework which change the shape of popular participation. As we shall see, these possibilities do occur, and are important. For much of the time however we must expect an entropy of democracy. It then becomes important to understand the forces at work within this and to adjust our approach to political participation to it. That is why I have called this pamphlet 'coping with' post-democracy, not reversing or overcoming it.

In the following discussion I try to explore some of the deeper causes of the phenomenon, and then ask what we can do about it. First however we must look in more detail at doubts which many will still entertain at my initial statement that all is not well with the state of our democracy.

Democratic crisis? What crisis?

It can be argued against me that democracy is currently enjoying one of its most splendid periods. Within the past quarter century we have seen: the final fall of fascist regimes in western Europe (Greece, Portugal and Spain); the gradual stabilisation of democratic regimes in much of Latin America and isolated parts of the Far East; the collapse of apartheid in South Africa; and, most spectacularly, the crash of communist dictatorships through eastern and central Europe.

Closer to home, within the so-called advanced countries, the argument continues, politicians receive less deference and uncritical respect from the public and mass media than perhaps ever before. Government and its secrets are increasingly laid bare to the democratic gaze. There are insistent and often successful calls for more open government and for constitutional reforms to make governments more responsible to the people. Surely, we today live in a more democratic age than in my 'democratic moment' of the third quarter of the 20th century; politicians were then trusted and respected by naive and deferential voters in a way that they did not deserve. What seems from one perspective to be manipulation of opinion by today's politicians can be viewed from another as politicians so worried about the views of a subtle and complex electorate that they have to devote enormous resources to discovering what it thinks, and then respond anxiously to it. Surely it is an advance in democratic quality that politicians are today more afraid than their predecessors to shape the political agenda, preferring to take much of it from the findings of market research techniques and opinion polls.

This optimistic view of current democracy has nothing to say about the fundamental problem of the power of corporate elites. This is the theme which I want to place at the centre of concern in the following sections of this pamphlet. But there is also an important differences between two concepts of the active democratic citizen, which is not recognised in optimistic discussions. On the one hand is positive citizenship, where groups and organisations of people together develop collective identities, perceive the interests of these identities, and autonomously formulate demands based on them, which they pass on to the political system. On the other hand is the negative activism of blame and complaint, where the main aim of political controversy is to see politicians called to account, their heads placed on blocks, and their public and private integrity held up to intimate scrutiny.

Democracy needs both of these approaches to citizenship, but at the present time the negative is receiving considerably more emphasis than the positive. This is worrying, because it is obviously positive citizenship which represents democracy's creative energies. The negative model, for all its aggression against the political class, shares with the passive approach to democracy the idea that politics is essentially an affair of elites, who are then subjected to blaming and shaming by an angry populace of spectators when we discover that they got something wrong. Paradoxically, every time that we regard a failure or disaster as being somehow resolved when a hapless minister or official is forced to resign, we connive at a model which regards government and politics as the business of small groups of elite decision-makers alone.

Alternatives to electoral politics

First however we must ensure that we have not hastily dismissed the importance of the lively world of causes and pressure groups which are probably growing in importance. Do these not constitute evidence of a healthy positive citizenship? Am I not in danger of concentrating too much on politics in the narrow sense of party and electoral struggle, and ignoring the displacement of creative citizenship away from this arena to the wider one of cause groups? Organisations on behalf of human rights, the homeless, the Third World, the environment and many other causes could be said to provide a far richer democracy, because they enable us to choose highly specific causes, whereas working through a party requires us to accept a whole package. Further, the range of objects of action available becomes far more extensive than just helping politicians get elected. And modern means of communication like the internet make it ever easier and cheaper to organise and co-ordinate new cause groups.

This is a very serious argument and, as we shall see in the final section, within it lie some of the answers to our present predicament. However, it also embodies some weaknesses. We need first to distinguish between those cause activities which pursue an essentially political agenda, seeking to secure action or legislation or spending by public authorities, and those which tackle tasks directly and ignore politics. (Of course, some groups in the former category may also do the latter, but that is not the issue here.)

Cause groups which set their face against political engagement have grown considerably in recent times. This is partly itself a reflection of the malaise of democracy and widespread cynicism about its capacities. This is particularly the case in the USA, where left-wing disgust at the monopolisation of politics by big business interests joins right-wing rejection of big government to celebrate non-political civic virtue. In the UK too there has been a major and highly diverse growth of self-help groups, communitarian networks, neighbourhood watch schemes, and charitable activities trying desperately to fill the gaps in care left by a retreating welfare state. Interesting, valuable, worthy though most of these developments are, precisely because they involve turning away from politics, they cannot be cited as indicators of the health of democracy, which is by definition political. Indeed, such activities can flourish in non-democratic societies, where political involvement is either dangerous or impossible, and where the state is particularly likely to be indifferent to social problems.

More complex are the second type of cause organisations: politically oriented campaigns and lobbies which, though not seeking to influence or organise votes, do work directly to affect government policy. Vitality of this kind is evidence of a strong liberal society; but this is not the same as a strong democracy. Since we have become so accustomed to the joint idea of liberal democracy we tend today not to see that there are two separate elements at work. Democracy requires certain rough equalities in a real capacity to affect political outcomes by all citizens. Liberalism requires free, diverse and ample opportunities to affect those outcomes. These are related and mutually dependent conditions. Maximal democracy certainly cannot flourish without strong liberalism. But the two are different things, and at points even conflict.

The difference was well understood in 19th century England, which was a liberal society but not a democratic one. And many liberals were acutely aware of a tension: the more that there was insistence on the criterion of equality of political capacity, the more likely was it that rules and restrictions would be developed to reduce inequalities, threatening liberalism's insistence on free and multiple means of action.

Take a simple and important example. If no restrictions are placed on the funds which parties and their friends may use to promote their cause and on the kinds of media resources and advertising which may be purchased, then parties favoured by wealthy interests will have major advantages in winning elections. Such a regime favours liberalism but hinders democracy, because there is nothing like a level playing field of competition as required by the equality criterion. This is the case with US politics. State funding for parties, restrictions of spending on campaigns, rules about buying time on television for political purposes, help ensure rough equality and therefore assist democracy, but at the expense of curtailing liberty. This is the case with many western European political systems.

The world of politically active causes, movements and lobbies belongs to liberal rather than to democratic politics, in that few rules govern the modalities for trying to exercise influence. The resources available to different causes vary massively and systematically. Lobbies on behalf of business interests always have an enormous advantage, for two separate reasons. First, they can always claim that unless government listens to them their firm or sector will not be successful, which jeopardises government's core concern with economic success. Second, they can wield enormous funds for their lobbying, not just because they are rich to start with, but because the success of lobbying will bring increased profits to the business: the lobbying costs constitute investment. Non-business interests can rarely claim anything so potent as damage to economic success; and the success of their lobbying will not bring material reward (this is true by definition of a non-business interest), so their costs represent expenditure, not investment.

Those who argue that they can work best for, say, healthy food, by setting up a cause group to lobby government and ignore party politics, must remember that the food and chemicals industries will bring battleships against their rowing boats. A flourishing liberalism certainly enables all manner of causes, good and bad, to seek political influence, and makes possible a rich array of public participation in politics. But unless it is balanced by healthy democracy in the strict sense it will always proceed in a systematically distorted way. Of course, electoral party politics is also disfigured by the inequalities of funding produced by the role of business interests. But the extent to which this is true depends on how much of liberalism is permitted to leak into democracy. The more that a level playing field is ensured in such matters as party funding and media access, the more true the democracy. On the other hand, the more that the modalities of liberal politicking flourish while electoral democracy atrophies, the more vulnerable the latter becomes to distorting inequalities and the weaker the democratic quality of the polity. A lively world of cause groups is evidence that we have the potential to come closer to maximal democracy. But this cannot be fully evaluated until we examine what use post-democratic forces are also making of the opportunities of liberal society.

The symptoms of post-democracy

If we have only two concepts—democracy and un-democracy—we cannot take discussion about the health of democracy very far. The idea of post-democracy helps us describe situations when boredom, frustration and disillusion have settled in after a democratic moment; when powerful minority interests have become far more active than the mass of ordinary people in making the political system work for them; where political elites have learned to manage and manipulate popular demands; where people have to be persuaded to vote by top-down publicity campaigns. This is not the same as non-democracy, but describes a period in which we have, as it were, come out the other side of the parabola of democracy. There are many symptoms that this is occurring in contemporary Britain and other advanced societies, constituting that we are indeed moving further away from the maximal ideal of democracy towards the post-democratic model. To pursue this further we must look briefly at the use of 'post-' terms in general.

The idea of 'post-' is thrown around rather easily in contemporary debate: post-industrial, post-modern, post-liberal, post-ironic. However, it can mean something very precise. Essential is the idea of an historical parabola through which the thing being attached to the 'post-' prefix can be seen as moving. This will be true whatever one is talking about, so let us first talk abstractly about 'post-X'. Time period 1 is pre-X, and will have certain characteristics associated with lack of X. Time period 2 is the high tide of X, when many things are touched by it and changed from their state in time 1. Time period 3 is post-X. This implies that something new has come into existence to reduce the importance of X by going beyond it in some sense; some things will therefore look different from both time 1 and time 2. However, X will still have left its mark; there will be strong traces of it still around. More interestingly, the decline of X will mean that some things start to look rather like they did in time 1 again. 'Post-' periods should therefore be expected to be very complex.

Post-democracy can be understood in this way. At one level the changes associated with it give us a move beyond democracy to a form of political responsiveness more flexible than the confrontations that produced the ponderous compromises of the mid-century years. To some extent we have gone beyond the idea of rule by the people to challenge the idea of rule at all. This is reflected in the shifting balance within citizenship referred to above: the collapse of deference to government, and in particular by the treatment of politics by the mass media, the insistence on total openness by government; and the reduction of politicians to something more resembling shopkeepers than rulers, anxiously seeking to discover what their 'customers' want in order to stay in business.

The political world then makes its own response to the unattractive and subservient position in which these changes threaten to place it. Unable to return to earlier positions of authority and respect, unable to discern easily what demands are coming to it from the population, it has recourse to the well known techniques of contemporary political manipulation, which give it all the advantages of discovering the public's views without the latter being able to take control of the process for itself. It also

13

imitates the methods of other worlds which have a more certain and self-confident sense of themselves: show business and the marketing of goods.

From this emerge the familiar paradoxes of contemporary politics: both the techniques for manipulating public opinion and the mechanisms for opening politics to scrutiny become ever more sophisticated, while the content of party programmes and the character of party rivalry becomes ever more bland and vapid. One cannot call this kind of politics non- or anti-democratic, because so much of it results from politicians' anxieties about their relations with citizens. At the same time it is difficult to dignify it as democracy itself, because so many citizens have been reduced to the role of manipulated, passive, rare participators.

It is in this context that we can understand remarks made by certain leading New Labour figures concerning the need to develop institutions of democracy going beyond the idea of elected representatives in a parliament, and citing the use of focus groups as an example. The idea is preposterous. A focus group is entirely in the control of its organisers; they select the participants, the issues, and the way in which they are to be discussed and the outcome analysed. However, politicians in a period of post-democracy confront a public which is confused and passive in developing its own agenda. It is certainly understandable that they should see a focus group as a more scientific guide to popular opinion than the crude and inadequate devices of their mass party claiming to be the voice of the people, which is the alternative historically offered by the labour movement's model of democracy.

The idea of an appointed second chamber, which has become the de facto policy of the Labour government for the House of Lords, is, far more clearly than focus groups, an offence to democracy. But within post-democracy it makes a certain sense.

Given declining participation in all elections, with those for the European parliament and local councils reaching very low levels, there seems little demand among people for more opportunities to vote. From the nomination process will emerge a house largely comprising wealthy businessmen, with significant sprinklings of women in general and men and women from the professions, trade unions and ethnic minorities.

But these representative figures are chosen as individuals and are not responsible in any real sense to those whom they are deemed to represent. These latter remain just the passive categories from whom prominent individuals are drawn to prevent the categories feeling excluded. This corresponds very closely to the ideal of representation of interests in the post-democratic polity. The active engagement of the ordinary population is not wanted, because it might become unmanageable; but their feeling excluded is also feared, as that might lead them into equally unmanageable rebellion, or at least to an indifference which undermines the legitimacy of those elected to rule.

Virtually all the formal components of democracy survive within post-democracy, which is compatible with the complexity of a 'post-' period. However, we should expect to see some erosion in the longer term, as we move, blasé and disillusioned, further and further away from maximal democracy. In Britain we can see stirrings of this in both Conservative and New Labour approaches to local government, the functions of which are gradually disappearing into either central government agencies or private firms. We should also expect the removal of some fundamental supports of democracy and therefore a parabolic return to some elements characteristic of pre-democracy. The globalisation of business interests and fragmentation of the rest of the population does this, shifting political advantage away from those seeking to reduce inequalities of wealth and power in favour of those wishing to return them to levels of the pre-democratic past.

Coping with post-democracy

Some of the consequences of this can already be seen. The welfare state is gradually becoming residualised as something for the deserving poor rather than a range of universal rights of citizenship; trade unions exist on the margins of society; the role of the state as policeman and incarcerator returns to prominence; the wealth gap between rich and poor grows; taxation becomes less redistributive; politicians respond primarily to the concerns of a handful of business leaders whose special interests are allowed to be translated into public policy; the poor gradually cease to take any interest in the process whatsoever and do not even vote, returning voluntarily to the position they were forced to occupy in pre-democracy. The most advanced and powerful society on earth today, the USA, already demonstrates the shift towards these characteristics more than any other. That the world's most future-oriented society should also be the one to show the strongest return to an earlier time is only explicable in terms of the parabola of democracy.

There is profound ambiguity in the post-democratic tendency towards growing suspicion of politics and the desire to submit it to close regulation, again seen most prominently in the USA. An important element of the democratic moment was the popular demand that the power of government should be used to challenge concentrations of private power. An atmosphere of cynicism about politics and politicians, low expectations of their achievements, and close control of their scope and power therefore suits the agenda of those wishing to rein back the active state, as in the form of the welfare state and Keynesian state, precisely in order to liberate and deregulate that private power. At least in western societies, unregulated private power was as much a feature of pre-democratic societies as unregulated state power.

Post-democracy also makes a distinctive contribution to the character of political communication. If one looks back at the

16

different forms of political discussion of the inter- and post-war decades one is surprised at the relative similarity of language and style in government documents, serious journalism, popular journalism, party manifestos and politicians' public speeches. There were certainly differences of vocabulary and complexity between a serious official report designed for the policy-making community and a tabloid newspaper, but compared with today the gap was small. Today the language of serious documents remains more or less similar to what it was then. But tabloid newspaper discussion and party manifestos are totally different. They rarely aspire to any complexity of language or argument. Someone accustomed to such a style suddenly requiring to access a document of serious debate would be at a loss as to how to understand it. Television news presentations, hovering uneasily between the two worlds, probably thereby provide a major service in helping people make such links.

Politicians' election broadcasts from the early post-war years seem comical when we view them now; but they are comical because these are people talking in the normal language of serious conversation, and with the mannerisms and quaintnesses that we all possess. This seems odd because we have become accustomed to hear politicians, not speaking like normal people, but presenting glib and finely honed statements which have a character all of their own. We call these 'sound bites', and having dismissively labelled them think no more about what is going on. Like the language of tabloid newspapers and party literature, this form of communication resembles neither the ordinary speech of the person in the street, nor the language of true political discussion. It is designed to be beyond the reach of scrutiny by either of these two main modes of democratic discourse.

This raises several questions. The mid-century population was on average less well educated than today's. Were they able to understand the political discussions presented to them? They certainly turned out for elections more consistently than their successors; and they regularly bought newspapers which addressed them at that higher level, paying for them a higher proportion of their incomes than we do today.

What then happened was as follows. Taken by surprise, first by the demand for, then by the reality of, democracy, politicians struggled for the first part of the 20th century to find means of addressing the new mass public. For a period it seemed that only men like Hitler, Mussolini and Stalin had discovered the secret of power through mass communication. Democratic politicians were placed on roughly equal discursive terms with their electorates through the clumsiness of their attempts at mass speech. Then the US advertising industry began to develop its skills, with a particular boost coming from the development of commercial television. The persuasion business was born as a profession. By far the dominant part of this remained devoted to the art of selling goods and services, but politics and other users of persuasion tagged along eagerly behind, extrapolating from the innovations of the advertising industry and making themselves as analogous as possible to the business of selling products so that they could reap maximum advantage from the new techniques.

We have now become so accustomed to this that we take it for granted that a party's programme is a 'product', and that politicians try to 'market' us their message. But it is not really at all obvious. Other successful models of how to talk to large numbers of people were potentially available among religious preachers, school teachers, serious popular journalists like George Orwell. Instead popular journalism ceased to follow the Orwellian pattern and, like politics, began to model itself on advertising copy: very brief messages requiring extremely low concentration spans; the use of words to form high-impact images instead of arguments appealing to the intellect. Advertising is not a form of rational dialogue. It does not build up a case based on evidence, but associates its products with a particular imagery. You cannot answer it back. Its aim is not to engage in discussion but to persuade to buy. Adoption of its methods has helped politicians to cope with the problem of communicating to a mass public; but it has not served the cause of democracy itself.

A further form taken by the degradation of mass political communication is the growing personalisation of electoral politics. Promotion of the claimed charismatic qualities of a party leader, and pictures and film footage of his or her person striking appropriate poses, increasingly take the place of debate over issues and conflicting interests. This kind of activity is also characteristic of dictatorships and of electoral politics in societies with weakly developed systems of parties and debate. With occasional exceptions (like Charles de Gaulle) it was much less prominent during the democratic moment; its insistent return now is another aspect of the parabola.

In addition to being an aspect of the decline from serious discussion, the recourse to show business for ideas of how to attract interest in politics, the growing incapacity of modern citizens to work out what their interests are, and the increasing technical complexity of issues, the personality phenomenon can be explained as a response to some of the problems of post-democracy itself. Although no-one involved in politics has any intention of abandoning the advertising industry model of communication, identification of specific cases of it, in current jargon stigmatised as 'spin', is tantamount to an accusation of dishonesty. Politicians have thereby acquired a reputation for deep untrustworthiness as a personality characteristic. The increasing exposure of their private lives to media gaze, as blaming, complaining and investigating replace constructive citizenship, has the same consequence. Electoral competition takes the form of a search for individuals of character and integrity. The search is futile because a mass election does not provide data on which to base such assessments. Instead what occurs is that politicians promote images of their personal wholesomeness and integrity, while their opponents only intensify the search through the records of their private lives to find evidence of the opposite.

Exploring post-democracy

In the sections that follow I shall explore both the causes and the political consequences of the slide towards post-democratic politics. The causes are complex. I have suggested that an entropy of maximal democracy has to be expected, but the question then arises of what emerges to fill the political vacuum which this creates. Today the most obvious force at work to do this has been economic globalisation. Large corporations have frequently outgrown the governance capacity of individual nation states. If they do not like the regulatory or fiscal regime in one country, they threaten to move to another, and increasingly states compete in their willingness to offer favourable conditions as they need the investment. Democracy has simply not kept pace with capitalism's rush to the global. The best it can manage are certain international groupings of states, but even the most important by far of these, the European Union, is a clumsy pygmy in relation to the agile corporate giants. And anyway its democratic quality, even by minimal standards, is weak. I shall take up some of these themes in Chapter 2, where we shall consider the limitations of globalisation as well as the importance of a separate but related phenomenon: the rise of the firm as an institution, its implications for the typical mechanisms of democratic government, and therefore its role in bending the parabola.

Alongside the strengthening of the global firm and firms in general has been a weakening of the political importance of ordinary working people. This partly reflects occupational changes which will be discussed in Chapter 3. The decline of those occupations which generated the labour organisations which powered the rise of popular political demands has left us with a fragmented, politically passive population which has not generated organisations to articulate its demands. More than that, the decline of Keynesianism and of mass production has reduced the economic importance of the mass of the population: the parabola of working-class politics.

These changes in the political place of major social groupings have important consequences for the relationship between political parties and the electorate. This is particularly relevant to parties of the left, which historically have represented the groups now being pushed back to the margins of political importance; but since many of the problems concern the mass electorate in general the issue extends much wider. Models of parties developed for coping with the rise of democracy have gradually and subtly been transformed into something else, the post-democratic party. This is the subject of Chapter 4.

Fabian pamphlets should always end with policy proposals to tackle the problems they have raised, usually addressed to the Labour Party. But one of the central problems raised by this pamphlet is whether parties are any longer available as addressees of policy proposals from egalitarians. Further, it is not the stance of this pamphlet to say: 'There are problems with democracy; what government policies might improve the situation?' My addressees are not members of any political elite, but troubled egalitarians who want to be positive, active citizens and not just the carping, passive spectators of what elites do. Therefore in the final section I ask: 'Given that there are problems with democracy, what can we, concerned citizens, do about it ourselves?'

2 | The global firm: the key institution of the post-democratic world

For most of the 20th century, socialists completely failed to appreciate the significance of the firm as an institution. Initially it seemed to them to be solely a device for reaping profits for owners and exploiting workers. The advantages of market sensitivity to consumers' demands that the firm embodied were largely lost on the generally poor working class who had only limited chances to express consumer preferences. Then, in the easy years of growing affluence of the third quarter of the 20th century, when mass consumerism began to take hold, the firm could be taken for granted as a convenient milch cow.

During this Keynesian period virtually all parties emphasised macro-economic policy. Individual companies were assumed to have no difficulty exploring and exploiting niches in product markets which were kept buoyant by the macro-policies. Those of the neo-liberal right who stressed the primacy of micro-economics and the problems of the firm were largely disregarded. In some ways this suited firms themselves: in setting a context of economic stability and not becoming involved in the fine details of what firms did, governments did not intervene much in their affairs.

The collapse of the Keynesian paradigm amid the inflationary crises of the 1970s changed all this. As aggregate demand levels were no longer guaranteed, product markets became unreliable.

This was intensified by other changes: rapid technological change and innovation; intensifying global competition; and more demanding consumers. Companies which had jogged along unenterprisingly found the ground cut from their feet. Differences between the successful and the unsuccessful became exaggerated; bankruptcies and unemployment grew. The survival of only reasonably successful firms could no longer be taken for granted. Lobbies and pressure groups working for the interests of the corporate sector were more likely to be listened to, just as complaints about a draught from an invalid have to be taken more seriously than those from a healthy person.

A number of other changes followed which, while they made the firm into a robust and demanding creature, anything but an invalid, continued paradoxically to have the same consequence of enforcing increased attention to its demands. It is becoming a cliché of political debate that globalisation has been fundamental to this. It obviously intensifies competition, and this exposes the vulnerabilities of individual firms. But the survivors of this competition are those who become tough, and the toughness is expressed, not just or even primarily against competitors, but against governments and work forces. If the owners of a global firm do not find a local fiscal or labour regime congenial, they will threaten to go elsewhere. They can therefore have access to governments, and influence the policies being pursued by them far more effectively than can its nominal citizens, even if they do not live there, have formal citizen rights there, or pay taxes. In *The New Wealth of Nations* (New York: Vintage Books, 1991) Robert Reich wrote about both this group and the highly paid professionals whose skills are demanded across the world, and the problems posed by the fact that they have considerable power but owe loyalty to no particular human community. Similar options are not available to the mass of the population, who remain more or less rooted to their native nation state, whose laws they must obey and taxes they must pay.

In many respects this resembles the situation in pre-revolutionary France, where the monarchy and aristocracy were exempt from taxation but monopolised political power, while the middle classes and peasantry paid taxes but had no political rights. The manifest injustice of this provided much of the energy and ferment behind the initial struggle for democracy. The global corporate elite does nothing so blatant as taking away our right to vote. (We are in the parabola of democracy, not coming full circle.) It merely points out to a government that, if it persists in maintaining, say, extensive labour rights, they will not invest in the country. All major parties in that country, fearing to call their bluff, tell their electorates that outmoded labour regulation must be reformed. The electorate then, whether conscious of the deregulation proposal or not, duly votes for those parties, there being few others to choose from. Deregulation of the labour market can be said, have been freely chosen by the democratic process.

Similarly, firms might insist on reduced corporate taxation if they are to continue to invest in a country. As governments oblige them, the fiscal burden shifts from firms to individual tax-payers, who in turn become resentful of high tax levels. The major parties respond to this by conducting general elections as tax-cutting auctions; the electorate duly favours the party offering the biggest tax cuts, and a few years later discovers that its public services have severely deteriorated. But they had voted for it; the policy had democratic legitimacy.

We must be careful not to exaggerate all this. The image of totally footloose capital is a curiously shared distortion of the left and the right. The former use it to present a picture of business interests totally out of control. The latter use it to argue against all measures of labour regulation and taxation that corporations find irksome. In reality, not only are many firms far from global, but even transnational giants are constrained by their existing patterns of investment, expertise and networks from skipping around the world in search of the lowest taxes and worst labour conditions. There was a sharp reminder of this during 2000, when both BMW and Ford decided to reduce their operations in Britain in favour of their German plants. Although an important part of the argument concerned the excessive strength of sterling, another was that it was more difficult and costly to close down an operation in Germany. In other words, the very efforts which Conservative and New Labour governments had made to attract inward investment by stressing how flexible British regulations were, made it more likely that inward investing firms would close a British factory. Easy come meant easy go.

However, while an economy like the German one might be more likely than the British to retain its existing manufacturing activities, the British stance might be more likely to attract more new firms, provided it continues to offer footloose global firms what they say they want. If this policy is so successful, gradually all countries will start to imitate it, competing with each other to offer inward investors everything they ask for, leading to the predicted 'race to the bottom' in labour standards, taxation levels and hence quality of public services (apart from those like roads and labour skills directly wanted by the inward investors). So far this race has been slow to develop, largely because pro-labour and pro-welfare interests in some (though by no mans all) European Union countries have retained more power than in the UK. Gradually however this could well erode. Whatever aspirations might emerge from the democratic processes of politics, a population needing employment has to bend the knee to global companies' demands.

Exaggerated or not, globalisation clearly contributes to the constraints imposed on democracy, which is a system that has difficulty rising above national levels. But the implications of the rising importance of the firm as an institution, which is one aspect of the globalisation question, go considerably further and have negative implications for democracy of a subtler kind.

The phantom firm

During the 1980s many large corporations tried to develop a company culture, or 'whole company' approach. This meant shaping everything about them for targeted pursuit of competitive success. In particular, the personalities of their employees and the quality of their loyalty to the organisation should be fashioned according to a central plan. This was the period when Japan was seen as the prime model of economic success, and large Japanese corporations had pursued such strategies particularly effectively. For many firms this became an argument why they should not allow external trade unions to represent their workers, or employers' associations to represent their own interests in collective bargaining, or even trade associations their more technical and marketing interests. They must be free to act and lobby for themselves.

This helped set the stage of the new prominence of the individual firm, but its subsequent development took a curious path. Enthusiasm for corporate cultures has been countered by two new master tendencies, which have followed the replacement of the Japanese by the US corporate model as the one which everyone is seeking to imitate: (i)the tendency for firms to change their identity very rapidly as they engage in takeovers, mergers and frequent reorganisations; (ii)the growing casualisation of the work force (including such developments as temporary labour contracts, franchising and the imposition of self-employed status on people who are de facto employees).

These changes are a response to what has become the overwhelming demand of firms: flexibility. This has been made their central operational priority by a combination of the uncertainty of today's markets and the new centrality of stock exchanges following global financial deregulation. Maximising shareholder value has become the overriding objective, and this requires a capacity to switch activities rapidly. Having full flexibility of this kind goes beyond the now familiar process of retaining a core business but sub-contracting ancillary activities. Having a core business itself becomes a rigidity. The most advanced firms outsource and sub-contract more or less everything except a strategic headquarters financial decision-making capacity. Information technology is of great assistance to them in the complex organisation tasks which this involves. The internet can be used both to assemble orders from customers and to commission production and distribution from a disaggregated set of production units, which can be rapidly changed from time to time. The object of a successful firm is to locate itself primarily in the financial sector, because this is where capital is at its most mobile, and to sub-contract everything else it does to small, insecure units.

The bewildering pace of mergers, and the phantom character of firms which constitute temporary, anonymous financial accumulations for the electronic co-ordination of a mass of disaggregated activities leads many commentators to see here the final dissolution of capital as a socio-political category, a major stage in the end of the class divisions of old industrial society. The early 21st century firm can thus seem a weaker institution than its predecessors: no longer the solid organisation with a large headquarters building and strong presence, but a soft, flexible, constantly changing will-o'-the-wisp.

Nothing could be further from the truth. Its capacity to deconstruct itself is the most extreme form taken by the firm's dominance of contemporary society. The classic firm had more or less stable ownership concentrations, a work force of dependent employees which it often encouraged to acquire long service, and a reputation with customers which it acquired over a prolonged period. The archetypical contemporary firm is owned by a constantly changing constellation of asset holders, who trade their shares in it electronically. It makes use of a diversity of labour-service contract forms in order to bring together fluctuating combinations of workers and dispense with the need to have any actual employees. Those who work for it are rarely in a position to identify and target it. Rather than seeking a reputation for quality for its products, it frequently changes its name and range of activities, using advertising and marketing techniques to acquire temporary images, which can in turn be replaced and re-engineered after a relatively short period. Customers have difficulty in establishing its track record. Invisibility becomes a weapon.

Behind the fluctuations two things remain. First, the identity of the major real owners of corporate wealth changes far more slowly: it is the same groups, more or less the same individuals, who keep appearing in new shapes and guises. The two economies which demonstrate the new form of flexible capitalism in the most advanced degree, the UK and the USA, are also the two advanced societies which are experiencing increasing inequality in property ownership, despite far wider nominal share ownership than in the past. Individual bundles of capital might deconstruct themselves, but not the ultimate owners. Second, however much individual firms may change their identity, the general concept of the firm as an institution acquires—partly as a result of this flexibility itself—greater prominence within society. This requires closer scrutiny, as it raises some major issues of post-democracy.

The firm as an institutional model

In many ways the flexible phantom firm is highly responsive to customers' wants. If one firm finds that it can maximise its profits by moving out of the construction of steel products and into the manufacture of mobile phones, another is likely to take its place in the former activity. This is the creative turmoil of the market. However, not all wants are best served by such a model. There may be strong reasons for ensuring that everyone should have access to certain facilities which it will be unprofitable for all firms within a completely free market. This is a familiar problem, to which the normal answer is that this indicates the role of government. But to acknowledge this requires acceptance that the modus operandi of government and private firm differ in certain respects. As a general principle this is widely accepted.

To take just one simple example: supermarkets place themselves on major out-of-town traffic routes where the majority of profitable customers can gain access to them. This leaves a residuum of people who find it very difficult to go shopping, but these are poor people whose small purchases it is not worth the supermarkets' while to bother about. This is sometimes considered a minor scandal, but this is small compared with what would happen in the following case. Imagine that a local education authority announces that, as part of its policy of market testing and best value procedures, it has been taking lessons in cost-effective location from consultants to supermarket chains. Henceforth it will be closing most of its schools and will reopen a small number of very large ones, located on motorway access points. Research has shown it that the small number of pupils whose parents do not have cars are likely to be poor educational performers. Therefore, in addition to considerable cost savings resulting from the closure of many schools, the county's scores in school league tables will improve as a result of the inability of these poorly performing children to attend school.

Everyone can think of many reasons why this is unacceptable and never practised. In doing so one makes use of concepts like the need for universal access to essential public services, which mark out the essential differences between public service and commercial provision. Government is however increasingly incapable of spelling out where the boundaries of these two lie. At moments of need, appeal will be made back to ideas of public service and citizen entitlement, forged some time between the late 19th and mid 20th centuries. But the relationship of these ideas, held in static veneration as museum pieces, and the new bustling forces of the commercialisation of government, which are the focus of virtually all new thinking and policy initiatives for service delivery within government, is rarely formulated coherently or even examined. There is real conflict here, and it is being glossed over, because governments envy the phantom firm its flexibility and apparent efficiency, and try to imitate it almost heedlessly.

Government increasingly renounces any distinctive role for public service (which stresses a duty to provide citizens with more or less equal services to a high standard), and requires its departments to act as firms (which stresses a duty of providing a service to that quality which is required by the meeting of financial targets). To achieve this change, parts of the public service are either privatised or contracted out to firms, or, staying within the public sector, are required to act as though they were firms. Like the phantom firm, government is trying gradually to divest itself of all direct responsibilities for the conduct of public services. In this way it hopes to avoid dependence on the vagaries of real reputation. But in doing so it relinquishes its claim to the special functions that can be performed only by the public service. This further leads to the conclusion that persons from the private corporate sector should manage public services, as it is only their expertise which is relevant now.

When firms take over parts of government activity they follow their usual approach of high flexibility and mobility. They cherry-pick the profitable parts. They will offer to take over schools in areas where their activities will have high profile. They will take on the health insurance of low-risk persons. This leaves the public service to carry on the static, non-profitable tasks which do not fit the requirements of dynamic entrepreneurial activity, but which cannot be dropped unless major changes are made to the rights of citizenship. As a result these services become marginalised, repositories of low morale among staff and apparent proofs of the thesis that the public service can only do dreary, unprofitable things. Much the same happens when public welfare services are seen as services of last resort for the marginal poor; they acquire a reputation for poor quality. This even further enhances the prestige of those who run the private sector. A vicious spiral is in progress. In the UK it has been operating for over two decades now, and is coming to seem irreversible.

Undermining government self-confidence

A major consequence of all this is an extreme lack of confidence on the part of the public services that they can do anything well unless they are under the guidance of the corporate sector. Eventually this becomes self-justifying. As more and more state functions are subcontracted to the private sector, so the state begins to lose competence to do things which once it managed very well. Gradually it even loses touch with the knowledge necessary to understand certain activities. It is therefore forced to sub-contract further and then buy consultancy services. Government becomes a kind of institutional idiot, its every ill-informed move being anticipated in advance and therefore discounted by smart market actors. From this follows the core policy recommendation of contemporary economic orthodoxy: the state had best do nothing at all, beyond guaranteeing the freedom of the markets.

As government increasingly divests itself of autonomous competences, it concedes to neo-liberal ideology what had once been a powerful argument in favour of active government: the capacity of the actor at the centre to perceive what cannot be seen by individual firms. This had been a central rationale for Keynesian policies in the first place. The experience of the 1920s and 1930s showed that the market might by itself be unable to stimulate a recovery, but that the state might be able to do so. Today's assumptions about the poverty of the state's knowledge and its likely incompetence rule this out.

In this way government is tending to resolve itself into three parts: a number of activities which it tries increasingly to convert into market form; a dreary, residual, burdensome set of obligations which the private sector will not take off its hands; and an image-creating, purely political component. It is not surprising that government is coming to be seen as a mixture of incompetence to provide real services plus parasitic spinning and electioneering. In the USA such an image is now firmly established, and respect for and interest in politics are at an historical low. This is in itself a major set-back for democracy, but even that is not the end of the story.

The corporate elite and political power

Firms are not simply organisations, but concentrations of power. Their pattern of ownership produces concentrations of private wealth, and the more important firms become, the more important becomes the class of capital owners. Further, the great majority of firms are organised in a manner which gives considerable authority to their senior managers. This becomes increasingly the case as the Anglo-American model of the firm, concentrating all power on a chief executive responsible solely to shareholders, pushes out various other forms of capitalism which recognise a wider range of stakeholders. The more powerful the firm becomes as an organisational form, the more powerful become the individuals who occupy these positions.

They become even more powerful as government concedes to

them the organisation of its own activities and bows to the supe-
riority of their expertise. In addition to dominating the economy
itself, they become the class which also dominates the running of
government.

There is yet another consequence. As government withdraws
from the extensive funding role it acquired in the Keynesian and
social democratic period, so organisations operating in non-
profit areas turn elsewhere for financial sponsorship. As wealth
and power gravitate towards the corporate sector, this becomes
the main potential source of such sponsorship. This brings
persons from the business sector into powerful positions as they
decide what they might sponsor. This has now reached the point
where think tanks associated with the Labour Party have to find
firms willing to fund individual items of their policy research,
and even government advisory bodies increasingly depend on
company donations to fund their work.

The reason why some of these activities were not in the corporate sector in the first place was often precisely that it was
considered inappropriate. For example, there are clear problems
if pharmaceutical firms become the main sponsors of medical
research - but that is precisely what is happening as governments
encourage universities to rely increasingly on sponsorship rather
than public funding. In the past, corporations usually channelled
their support for scientific and cultural activity through trusts
managed quite autonomously from the firms themselves. This
was during the period of democratic sensitivities, when people
would look askance at direct involvement in what were seen as
non-commercial activities by centres of commercial power and
interest. Today sponsorship is less often mediated in this way,
and firms are likely to fund activities directly.

In order to encourage scientific, cultural and other non-
commercial activities to seek private sponsorship, governments
increasingly make their own financing of such activities

dependent on success in attracting such sponsorship: a local theatre or a university department will get public help if it can first make itself attractive to private donors. This further strengthens the power of wealthy people, enabling them to determine the allocation of public funds, as public money follows the allocative decisions made by the private sponsor. A similar example is the practice, originating in the USA but rapidly spreading, of permitting charitable donations to be offset against liability for taxation. The objective in doing this is to reduce the funding that government itself must undertake. Its consequence however is that wealthy corporations and individuals have been able, not only to decide which of a number of activities to favour with their own money, but simultaneously to pre-empt the pattern of public spending, which often originally existed precisely in order to assert priorities different from those which would be chosen by the rich.

A further consequence still of these developments is that entrepreneurs and company managers acquire very privileged access to politicians and civil servants. Since their success and expertise depend entirely on their ability to maximise value for their firms' shareholders, they must be expected to use that access for the benefit of those individual firms. This becomes particularly the case if, as is increasingly so in Britain, relations between government and an economic sector flow, not through associations representing firms in the sector, but through individual large corporations. Further, as government out-sources and sub-contracts ever more of its activities—usually doing so on the advice of persons from the corporate sector—so the potential value of such access in winning government contracts increases. If, as I argued in the previous chapter, one characteristic of current politics is a shift to the liberal model of lobbying and cause presentation as opposed to the politics of parties, this is a serious development. It suggests that the politics of the lobby will be shifting ever further towards the enhancement of the power of major corporations and those who hold powerful offices within them. The power that they already possess within their firms becomes translated into a far more extensive political power. This challenges severely the democratic balance.

These developments in the growing political power of corporate interests are often presented in terms of the superior efficiency of markets. This is richly ironic. A primary concern of the original 18th century formulations of free-market economic doctrines by Adam Smith and others was to disentangle the political world and private entrepreneurs from each other, combating in particular the granting of monopolies and contracts to court favourites. Much of the current activity of privatising, contracting out and breaking down the separateness of public service and private firms returns us precisely to that dubious behaviour. We therefore witness another aspect of the parabola: a return to corporate political privilege under slogans of markets and free competition.

These things can only happen in societies which have lost the sense of a distinction between a public interest, guarded by public authorities careful to establish their own autonomous competence, and private interests looking after themselves. In pre-democratic times social elites which dominated economic and social life also monopolised political influence and positions in public life. The rise of democracy forced them at least to share space in the latter arenas with representatives of non-elite groups. Today, however, through the growing dependence of government on the knowledge and expertise of corporate executives and leading entrepreneurs, and the dependence of parties on their funds, we are steadily moving towards the establishment of a new dominant, combined political and economic class. Not only do they have increasing power and wealth in their own right as societies become increasingly unequal, but they have acquired the privileged political role that has always been the mark of true dominant classes. This is the central crisis of early 21st century democracy.

There is a tendency in Britain to see classes in terms of their cultural attributes—accent, dress, typical leisure pursuits—and therefore to declare the passing of class society if a particular set of these seems to decline. A far more serious meaning of the term identifies connections between different types of economic position and differential access to political power. This is far from declining. Its return is one of the most serious symptoms of the move to post-democracy, as the rise of the corporate elite parallels the decline in the vigour of creative democracy. It also establishes the link between the two problems I established at the outset: the difficulties of egalitarian politics and the problems of democracy. One of the core political objectives of corporate elites is clearly to combat egalitarianism.

3 | Social class in post-democracy

The contemporary political orthodoxy that social class no longer exists is itself a symptom of post-democracy. In non-democratic societies, elite classes proudly display themselves and their power; democracy challenges class privileges; post-democracy denies their existence. The other aspect of class denial concerns the existence of subordinate classes. While this can be vigorously contested at an analytical level, it is certainly increasingly difficult for these classes to perceive themselves, or be perceived, as clearly defined social groups. This fact, and the imbalance produced by the combination of it with the growing self-awareness of the corporate elite, is a major cause of the problems of democracy.

The decline of the manual working class

By the end of the 19th century many skilled and some unskilled manual working groups had successfully organised themselves into trade unions. In Britain there was no once and for all struggle for suffrage as there had been in a number of continental European countries, the right to vote being very gradually extended to include growing numbers of male manual workers between 1868 and 1918. There was however considerable experience of political exclusion as newly enfranchised working-class interests tried to find those in the existing system willing to represent them. There was also a strong sense of social exclusion, most non-manual groups of the period regarding even skilled manual workers as unfit to be suitable social companions. These factors were reinforced by patterns of residential segregation that produced single-class communities within neighbourhoods in most industrial towns.

The divisions were never clear-cut, and other cleavages often proved more important: that between Anglicans and Non-conformists, for example, or between English natives and Irish immigrants. However, there was enough class-related political activity to make an impact. The working class's relative social exclusion meant that its discontent was constantly feared, and the poverty of parts of it made it a worrying social problem. From the end of the 19th century through to the third quarter of the 20th, finding ways of coping with the political existence of this class was the major preoccupation of domestic politics. For most of this time the class was growing in numbers, and eventually also in income, so that it began to have an effect on consumer markets as well as on policy for industrial relations and social welfare. It could plausibly be presented as the class of the future, and politicians of nearly all parties knew that their own futures depended on their ability to respond to its demands. Further, it was only when economies were reshaped to make possible working-class prosperity that the dynamism of mid 20th century mass-production capitalism took off.

Then, in the mid-1960s, the relative size of the manual working class began to decline. Increased productivity and automation reduced the numbers of production workers needed for a given unit of output, while employment in administrative support activities, as well as in the various service sectors (especially those associated with the welfare state) were growing steadily in size. The collapse of much manufacturing in the 1980s and new waves of technological change in the 1990s eroded direct industrial employment even further. While large numbers of people, mainly men, continued to be manual workers, the class was no longer the class of the future. By the end of the 20th century large parts of it were engaged in defensive, protectionist battles only, in the UK more than in most other advanced societies. The early stages of the decline had been marked by an industrial militancy that veered between mere defence and the construction of new strategic possibilities, though in Britain the former usually predominated. In the 1980s the final ferocious battle of organised labour, the miners' strike of 1984-85, was one of hopeless, self-destructive, last-ditch defence alone.

At the political level the Labour Party had been responding to the relative decline of the manual working class since at least the 1960s with some attempts to add various growing new non-manual groups to its coalition. This was particularly successful among men and women working in the public services, a major constituent of growth in non-manual employment at that time. The desperate leftward lurch of the party in the early 1980s however led it to forget its historical future-oriented role, and to attempt to forge coalitions of out-groups. In the deindustrialising north, in Liverpool, the party was forced back into a defiant proletarian redoubt—a strategy first and disastrously pursued by the French Communist Party. In the new cosmopolitan, post-modern south, in London, there were attempts to forge a non-class rainbow coalition of the excluded, bringing together ethnic minorities and various interests primarily concerned with sexual orientation; a path also followed at the time by the US Democratic Party.

Both Liverpool and London strategies were destined to fail. The manual working class had begun the century as the future battering on the door, representing the collective interest in an age damaged by individualism: it brought the message of universal citizenship, and the possibilities of mass consumption in a society that knew only luxury goods for the rich and subsistence for the poor. By the end it represented history's losers: advocacy of the welfare state began to take the form of special appeals for compassion, not universal demands for citizenship. During the course of a century the class had described its parabola.

The incoherence of other classes

It is more difficult to tell the class story of the rest—today the clear majority—of the population: the diverse and heterogeneous groups of professionals, administrators, clerical and sales workers, employees of financial institutions, of public bureaucracies and of welfare state organisations. Defined historically by education standards, incomes and working conditions superior to those of manual workers, most of these groups have often been reluctant to ally themselves to the interests and organisations of the working class. Most have however failed to generate much autonomous political profile at all. Occupational organisations are usually (with very important exceptions among the professions and public service employees) weak; voting behaviour is very mixed, lacking the clear biases of manual and true bourgeois classes.

This does not mean that people in these groups are apathetic about public life. On the contrary, as individuals they are the most likely to be found as active members of interest organisations and cause groups. But they are spread across a wide political spectrum of these, and therefore do not confront the political system with a clear agenda of demands—as does the resurgent capitalist class and once did the manual working class. They are often seen as politically closer to capital, in that in two-party systems they have tended historically to vote more for antisocialist than for labour-based parties. But their position is more complex than that; they are, for example, strong supporters of the citizenship welfare state, especially services for health, education and pensions.

Closer inspection enables us to see more definite patterns within this middle mass. There is often a public/private division, the former far more likely to be unionised and—rather obviously —to be involved in organisations and lobbies for the protection of public services. The privatisation of much of the public sector had an important electoral logic in the 1980s, when in Britain the Conservative Party was becoming one opposed to public employees and therefore seeking to reduce their numbers.

There are also major hierarchical divisions. Little or nothing connects routine office workers to senior managers, both the incomes and educational levels of the former often being lower than those of skilled manual workers. It is essential to recognise the role of gender here. In general, and of course with exceptions, the lower down a hierarchy, the lower the pay, and the lower the educational level that a non-manual worker exists, the more likely she is to be female. The gender divide provides at least as sharp a cultural cleavage within the non-manual hierarchy of the office or shop as the manual/non-manual one within the factory.

If one assumes that senior managerial and professional workers have good reasons to associate themselves with the political interests of capital—unless they work in the public services—the question why the lower ranks of the white-collar hierarchy have not developed a distinctive politics of their own becomes almost equivalent to the question: why did women not articulate an autonomous politics of the junior non-manual classes, in the way that men did for the skilled manual working class? This question is so important for the state of contemporary democracy that I will return to it in more detail below.

It will be objected to this account of the weakness of middle-Britain interests that if anything politicians are obsessed with this group and its concerns. However, these concerns are processed by the political system in a manner which defines them as entirely at one with those of business. This is what Conservatives have been doing for more than a century. If New Labour is successfully rivalling them in its appeal to middle Britain, it is simply because it has started doing the same, not because it is articulating wider concerns of these groups, which might be uncomfortable for the corporate elite. They are represented as having no discontents except with the quality of public services—which is increasingly taken to mean that they want these privatised. They are encouraged to seek no means of social improvement other than for themselves and their children obediently to climb the career ladders established by business elites. From this follows the obsessive concern of contemporary politics with education, as this seems to provide the most sure means of upward mobility. Since social mobility can only be enjoyed by a minority and in competition with everyone else, it is a very odd policy to offer as a general solution to life's discontents. It is probably for this reason that Conservatives and Labour alike have encouraged people to blame school teachers and local education authorities for the fact that every child is not the leader of the pack.

The relationship to politics of these middle-Britain groups therefore conforms closely to the post-democratic model of politics: it is in relation to them that manipulative politics is most used; the group itself remains largely passive and lacks political autonomy. This is unsurprising: these are the groups which have grown in numbers during the post-democratic period. Intriguingly, they are not part of a parabola. Non-manual workers have not experienced a past period of political exclusion, as their numbers were very small in the pre-democratic period; during the high-tide of democracy they played a passive part as the busy forces of big business and organised (largely manual) labour struggled to find the social compromise. As a result they do not experience much of a change with post-democracy.

Women and democracy

There has however been one major recent point of change and disruption to this model of passivity: the political mobilisation of women. The puzzle raised above of why there was historically little autonomous expression of women's political demands can be easily answered. First, women, as guardians of the family, the non-work sphere, were for long less inclined than men to shape their political outlook with reference to the workplace. They participated less in organisations of all kinds, except the church. For complex reasons that need not concern us here, in most European countries it has been conservative parties which have stood for these domestic and religious interests. Although large numbers of women have joined the work force during the past 30 years, the majority have done so part-time, so their particular connection to the domestic sphere—if no longer to the religious in a society as secularized as England—has only been partly attenuated.

Second, while men, as the gender active in public life as a matter of course, could set up unions and movements without anyone at the time regarding their male character as embodying some kind of attack on the female sex, for women the situation is very different. To articulate a feminine vision is to criticise a masculine one. Given that the majority of people relate to their wider society through their families, it is difficult for women to develop the specific interests of their distinctive occupational groups without causing domestic tension and with little hope of forming communities. It is no coincidence that specifically feminist organisations usually articulate the concerns of single women more effectively than they do those of married ones.

However, between the early 1970s and the present day this situation has begun to change. There has been a mobilisation, or rather a diversity of mobilisations, of female identities and their political expression. Alongside the green movement these have constituted the most important instances of democratic politics at work in its positive, creative sense. The development has followed the classic pattern of popular mobilisations. Starting with small groups of intellectuals and extremists, it spread to express itself in complex, rich and uncontrollable ways, but all rooted in the fundamental requirement of a great movement: the discovery of an unexpressed identity, leading to the definition of interests and the formation of formal and informal groups to give expression to these. As with all great movements, it took the existing political system by surprise and could not be easily manipulated. It also developed in ways out of control by official feminist movements. Feminist pioneers might not have had phenomena like Girl Power in mind when they sought to mobilise their sisters, but it is characteristic of a true major social movement that it takes a confusing and sometimes contradictory multiplicity of forms.

Extremist radicals, sober Fabian policy-makers, cunning reactionaries taking the movement's messages and reinterpreting them, both elite and popular cultural manifestations of many kinds, the gradual suffusion into the conversation of ordinary people of elements of the language of an initially esoteric movement: all the major accoutrements of a great democratic phenomenon have been present. Gradually too the political system started to respond and produce policies addressed to women's expressed concerns in a diversity of ways. Parallel to this ran an interest of political and business elites themselves in increasing female labour-force participation. The oddly poised and possibly unstable state of contemporary gender relations, where it seems to be widely assumed that both men and women will have jobs, but women will still be the main domestic carers, makes women ideal candidates for accepting part-time work; this suits the needs of firms for a flexible work force. And governments are also grateful for the increase in the number of taxpayers which female labour-force participation brings. But far from diminishing the importance of the movement, this only reinforces it. After all, the political rise of the manual working class was similarly accompanied by the growing dependence of the economy on its consumption power.

The capacity for political autonomy of women continues to be restrained by the factors mentioned above, but the whole experience has constituted a democratic moment within the overall framework of the onward march of post-democracy, reminding us that major historical tendencies can be contradicted.

The problem of New Labour

The position of New Labour can easily be understood from the perspective of the foregoing discussion. Its party's former social base had become associated with defensive decline and defeat, and no longer provided a viable launching point for accessing the future in either the electorate or substantive issues. The organisations which were supposed to ground the politicians in the concerns of the people—the Labour Party itself and its associated trade unions—became increasingly detached from growth points in the electorate, and gave completely misleading signals.

The achievement of New Labour was to shake off the impediment of this organisational albatross, but this has left it as a party with little in terms of distinctive social interests—with the highly significant exception of giving considerably greater attention than its Conservative and Labour predecessors to issues of importance to women, which is what the immediately preceding discussion should lead us to expect. This apart, the shift from Labour to New Labour can be read as the shift from a party suited to democratic politics to one prepared for post-democracy, through the nightmare transition of the 1980s as the democratic model ceased to be viable. This leaves the party free gradually to leave its base and become a party for all. But for a party to have no particular base is to exist in a vacuum. That is something which political nature abhors, and the newly confident corporate interests, embodied in the newly aggressive and flexible model of the share value maximising firm, have rushed to fill it. This explains the paradox of New Labour in government. Here was a new, refreshing, modernising force, oriented to change; but as its social and economic policy agenda emerged, it increasingly became a continuation of the preceding 18 Conservative years.

Meanwhile, a potential radical and democratic agenda remains unused. In the more purely market-oriented societies to which we are moving, income inequality, relative and even absolute poverty increase sharply. The new flexible labour markets make life very insecure for at least the bottom third of the working population. While the decline of manual work in manufacturing industry and coal-mining has reduced the proportion of work which is dirty and dangerous, much of the new service sector employment brings its own degradations. In particular, work in the rapidly growing personal services sector frequently involves a subordination of the person to employers and customers that has reintroduced many humiliating features of the old world of domestic service. Shoe-shine boys, baggage carriers and pedlars are back on the streets, all regarded as part of the jobs miracle and removed from the unemployment register.

Modern work problems are not just confined to the bottom third. Throughout the occupational structure people are finding that their jobs are taking up more and more of their lives and bringing them unreasonable stress. The down-sizing processes engaged in by most public and private sector organisations in recent years to cut staff costs have produced excessive work loads at many levels. In the UK and USA, after a century of gradual reductions, working hours are now lengthening. Since both men and women now work within the formal economy, there is less overall time for leisure and family life. This is happening in an age when parents need to devote increasing energy to steering their sons and daughters through an increasingly difficult childhood: pressures from various forms of deviance, and growing pressures from those areas of capitalism which have discovered that children are exceptionally soft touches as customers, compete with an increasingly frenzied need to do well educationally in order to keep one's nose in front of an occupational race which is increasing both its rewards to winners and its punishments to losers.

Politicians might argue that it has become increasingly difficult for the state to meet needs for protection from the market's vagaries, given the apparent reluctance of modern populations to pay taxes. But to argue that objectively these needs no longer exist, or could not be turned into issues of political concern by a political party seriously wanting to highlight them, is quite specious. The problems we experience at work remain high on any objective political agenda. And it could bring together new and old sections of the workforce. A party really seeking to represent the interest of these combined groups does not have far to look. The thorough reluctance of New Labour to engage in such possibilities demonstrates how far it has come in responding to the more powerful forces at work in post-democracy.

That New Labour has at least played with the idea of moving beyond the rapprochement and co-operation with business interests which is essential to all social democratic parties to becoming more or less a business party is evident at a number of points, not least the unusual relationships that came to light during 1998, linking many ministers, their advisors, firms of professional lobbyists who charge companies for access to ministers, and companies themselves. To the extent that some of these activities are concerned with finding sources of party funds from the business world to replace trade-union funding, they relate very directly to Labour's dilemma of seeking an alternative social base to the working class. The consequences are emerging at a number of points, joining the discussion of this chapter to that of the political rise of the corporate elite discussed in the previous one. It remains now to consider the implications of these changes for the internal structure of political parties.

4 | The political party under post-democracy

Political science textbooks usually model the relationship between parties and their wider electorates in terms of a series of related circles of growing size: the smallest comprises the leadership core, together with its advisors; next come parliamentary representatives; then active members, people who spend a lot of their time working actively for the party, as councillors, local activists, paid staff; next, ordinary members, who do little for the party, but want to have a symbolic attachment to it, help with the occasional activity, and pay a regular membership subscription; then supporters, or loyal voters, who do virtually nothing for the party except reliably turn out for it on election days; finally, the largest circle of all, the wider electorate, which the party seeks to persuade to vote for it.

In the pure model of a democratic party these circles are concentric: the leaders are drawn from the activists, who are drawn from the party membership, which is part of and therefore reflects the concerns and interests of those parts of the electorate which the party most seeks to represent. A major function of the intermediate circles is to link political leaders to the electorate in a two-way interaction via the various levels of the party.

Such a model is particularly important to the self-image of parties like the Labour Party or the Scottish and Welsh Nationalist Parties, parties which originated outside parliament as social movements and then developed a parliamentary arm. In recent decades however it has becomes increasingly important also for parties like the Conservatives and Liberals, who originated within the political elite and subsequently cast about to fabricate for themselves a national movement as the age of democracy crept up on them. Ironically these parties increasingly present themselves as movement parties in precisely the period when the advance of post-democracy makes their earlier model as a disembodied political elite more realistic.

Like all ideals, the democratic model of concentric circles never really exists. However, there can be movement towards or away from it at different times, and it is instructive to observe these. Tensions occur within any organisation basically resembling the democratic model when the leadership suspects that the activists are a very biased sample of even the loyal electorate; since they are self-selected, this is likely to be true. It can then be expected to use other methods of discovering voters' views. Until the mid-20th century and the invention of mass opinion polling this was difficult to do, and it was during this period that active members were able to establish their claim to interpret the voters' stances. Today matters are very different.

Tensions become even greater when leaderships believe that the support base provided by the loyal electorate is too small, and start casting around for votes in the pool of the general electorate. If this involves approaching groups alien to the concerns of the activists, and in no way concentric to the existing party, there will be conflict. If there is success in getting some of the new groups within the active membership, then the conflict takes place among activists themselves; if the new groups are tapped only by opinion polling and other non-membership methods, there is the possibility of a curious bond linking the innermost and outermost of the concentric circles, at the expense of all intermediate relationships.

The challenge of post-democracy

Recent changes, including those discussed in previous sections concerning the rise of the firm and the confusion of class structure, have had major implications for the concentric model. A further change has been the vast extension of circles of advisors and lobbyists around leaderships. Although three groups can be distinguished—leaders, advisors and lobbyists—in practice individuals move between these positions, and together comprise the specialised occupation of politics.

This process changes the shape of the leadership core in relation to the other party circles. It becomes an ellipse. This begins where it always did, with party leaders and activist professionals at the heart of the party, seeking as reward either advancement into the leadership or the psychic rewards of policy success. But there are also those who, even though sympathetic to the party and its goals, work for it primarily for money. Beyond them are pure professionals, who are hired by the party to do a job, and who may not necessarily be its political supporters. More important, all these groups overlap and interact with groups of lobbyists working for firms who have an interest in government business to establish contacts with politicians. As discussed in Chapter 2, a party in or eligible for government today is heavily involved in privatisation and sub-contracting. Links with government personnel can be vital for firms wanting to gain from this. Sub-contracting is the more important, because it usually relates to services close to the heart of policy, therefore unable to be fully privatised, and with contracts subject to periodic renewal. Firms wanting a share of this business are well advised to maintain permanent contact with the policy-making core of a governing party. Members of the firms spend periods within the advisory circles, and party advisors get jobs as lobbyists with the firms. In this, the inner core becomes stretched way beyond the party's ranks.

All parties experience this vulnerability. It lay behind many of the corruption scandals which affected the Thatcher and Major Conservative governments. Once the concept of what makes public service special has been held up to ridicule and destroyed, and the pursuit of personal profit has been elevated into the supreme human goal, it can only be expected that MPs, advisors and others will regard selling their political influence for gain as a major and totally legitimate aspect of their participation in political life.

Although New Labour is not sure how to define the distinctiveness of public service, it has certainly not gone so far as post-Thatcher Tories in failing to recognise boundaries between public service and private profit. On the other hand, the general problem of the elliptical political elite presents special difficulties for social democratic parties, as their membership and electoral cores are that much further removed from elites than are those of right-of-centre parties. Particularly problematic for Labour and some of its sister social democratic parties in other countries have been the consequences of changes in class structure discussed in Chapter 3. As the manual working class shrank, party activists who looked largely to that class became of diminishing use as links between leadership and wider electorate. The leadership naturally sought to escape being caught in this historical trap, and turned increasingly to expert channels for advice on public opinion. While tensions of this kind are endemic to the concentric model, at a period of major class change they can become unmanageable. The processes used to discover the opinions of new groups was top-down and passive; very little resulted from autonomous mobilisation by the groups themselves. The result was to move the structure of the leadership further from the circles of the party towards the ellipse.

The main historical value of activists to party leaderships has been their contribution to vote-gathering, either directly through their unremunerated time, or through financial contributions and fund-raising. The new extended ellipse tries to provide its own partial alternatives to this too. The firms which increasingly congregate around party leaderships can offer a party money which can be used in the national and particularly television campaigns which have largely replaced local activities for vote gathering.

From the point of view of a party leadership, relations with the new ellipse are much easier, better informed, and rewarding than those with the old circles of activists. The expertise of the ellipse is of far more use than the amateur enthusiasm which is all that the normal party activist has to offer. If we extrapolate from recent trends, the classic party of the 21st century would be one which comprises a self-reproducing inner elite, remote from its mass movement base, but nested squarely within a number of corporations, which will in turn fund the sub-contracting of opinion-polling, policy-advice and vote-gathering services, in exchange for being well regarded by the party when in government.

At present only one almost pure example of such a party exists, and it is a party of the right, not of social democracy: Forza Italia in Italy. Following the collapse through corruption scandals of the Christian Democratic and Socialist Parties in the early 1990s, the entrepreneur Silvio Berlusconi rapidly filled the vacuum which would otherwise have ensured an easy passage to government by the then Communist Party by pooling resources from his extensive network of enterprises: television channels, a publishing house, a major football club, a financial empire, a leading supermarket chain, etc. Within a matter of months the party had become one of the leading ones in the Italian state and, despite various vicissitudes largely resulting from corruption scandals, it has remained such. Initially, it had no members or activists at all as such. Many of the functions normally filled by volunteers were carried out by the employees of Berlusconi's various enterprises. Money was obviously not needed, and a man who owns three national television channels, a national newspaper and a popular weekly magazine does not need party activists to get his message across.

Forza Italia is an example of a political party produced by the forces identified in Chapter 2: it is essentially a firm, or network of firms, rather than an organisation of the classic party type; it did not emerge from any formulation of interests by social movements, but was a construction of parts of the existing political and financial elite. It is also based on the personality of its leader more than on any particular party programme. As noted in Chapter 1, this is itself highly characteristic of post-democracy.

However, the story of Forza Italia also shows us that the time is by no means yet fully ripe for a party totally of this new kind. As the years have passed, so it has come to resemble more closely a classic party: it has acquired members and a local voluntary structure, and it has become more successful as a result. The crucial element here has been the importance in Italy—far more than in the UK—of local government as the prime link between people and politics and as the lifeblood of parties. Forza Italia had to acquire local bases and actual members in order to have an actual and not just a virtual presence among the electorate, both day-to-day and for getting the vote out at election time. As it did this it started to achieve success in local politics to match its national presence—though partly by Berlusconi using his television stations to turn local elections into little more than a reflection of national politics, a novelty in Italy but long familiar in Britain.

That dispensing with party activists is premature can also be seen from the experience of New Labour. The party has made a major and successful effort to attract corporate funding to replace dependency on trade unions and the mass membership.

However, the new form of politics, with its dependency on extremely heavy mass media presentations and purchased professional services, is very expensive. Parties' needs for money have become enormous. One of the factors behind the recent rise in political corruption scandals in a number of leading countries, from Germany and Italy to Japan, has been the vast appetite for funds of contemporary election campaigns. It would be a foolhardy party which would try to shift away from dependence on members and unions to dependence on corporations, when it might instead receive money from both. Ironically, the very cost of professionalised electioneering sends parties back to the arms of the traditional activists. At present, all these forces co-exist uneasily and in mutual suspicion.

It was argued in the opening chapter that the post-democratic period combines characteristics of the democratic and pre-democratic periods as well as those distinctly its own. This is the case with the contemporary political party. The legacy of the democratic model survives and continues to play a vital part, though without much capacity to renew itself, in the continuing dependence of leaders on the concentric circles of the traditional mass party. The new ellipse running from the leadership through its consultants to external lobbies paradoxically constitutes both the post-democratic and pre-democratic part. It is post-democratic in so far as it is concerned with the opinion research and expert policy work characteristic of this period. It is pre-democratic in the way that it provides privileged political access for individual firms and commercial interests. The tensions within the contemporary party of the centre left are the tensions of post-democracy itself.

5 | Conclusions: Where do we go from here?

I have tried to show in the preceding discussions how the fundamental cause of democratic decline in contemporary politics is the major imbalance now developing between the role of corporate interests and those of virtually all other groups. Taken alongside the inevitable entropy of democracy, this is leading to politics once again becoming an affair of closed elites, as it was in pre-democratic times. The distortions operate at a number of levels: sometimes as external pressures exercised on governments, sometimes through internal changes within the priorities of government itself, sometimes within the very structure of political parties.

These changes are so powerful and widespread that it is impossible to see any major reversal of them. However, actions to try to shift contemporary politics partly away from the inexorable drift towards post-democracy are possible and can be propounded at three levels: policies for the reform of political practice as such; policies to tackle the growing dominance of the corporate elite; and actions available to concerned citizens themselves.

Improving democracy

Under the first heading comes a familiar list of policies which those worried at current political trends should support. For example, if we are concerned at the deterioration of the quality of electoral debate, we should support current moves at the Department for Education and Employment for adding studies in citizenship to the school curriculum. If the public demonstrated disgust at trivialisation by punishing those parties which addressed them through advertising imagery and rewarded those that spoke to them as adults, parties would very quickly adjust. The parties themselves cannot be expected to risk taking such a step; the public itself has to demand it. Higher overall standards of education have clearly not been an adequate force to achieve this. Would a generation of young people who acquired at school as much sophistication of political understanding as they have with computer skills behave any differently? We cannot know, but we should at least support the attempt.

We have also seen that, even if national party organisations have been removed into a new self-referential elite ellipse, at local level there is considerably more vitality because of the continuing role of ordinary activists in local government. Concerned egalitarians should therefore rush to support local government from the attacks currently being made on it. New Labour is extending the previous Conservative government's policy of privatising many local council functions. This process is in particular now affecting education authorities—whose work is perhaps the most important single issue for attracting Labour activists to local politics. Their powers are gradually being contracted out to private firms, or absorbed into the central state, and it cannot be taken for granted that, without major resistance, they will survive another parliament.

Moves for the direct election of mayors in some cities are ambiguous. They could weaken local parties further, since an explicit aim of this policy has been to open up local politics to non-party individuals, preferably those wealthy enough to fund their own campaigns and therefore likely to be drawn from very wealthy persons—a text-book instance of post-democratic politics. (The case of Ken Livingstone shows how policies can back-fire, but it does not change the general logic of the policy.) On the other hand, if mayors could be elected in ways which did not favour those with large personal assets but which reinforced the role of parties, their role might actually revive local politics.

The current position of English regional government resembles that of the new post-democratic House of Lords: appointed assemblies, drawn largely from corporate executives but with a sprinkling of individuals representative of certain categories of person, though not responsible to those categories in any organ-isational sense. If local government functions are shifted towards this new tier while it remains in this condition, local democracy will be further undermined. On the other hand, devolution in Northern Ireland, Scotland and Wales has been a recrudescence of democracy and a revitalisation of local politics—responding to autonomously generated social movements in the classic pattern of democratic politics. Can the English regional tier develop in a similar way?

A move to proportional representation would be the single biggest reform enabling the abandoned causes of the left in Britain to take advantage of the opportunities for more open and intensive political competition presented by post-democracy. This may seem a surprising conclusion, since such a reform is usually opposed by those who cling to a labour movement model appropriate to the politics of the democratic moment, the first-past-the-post system seeming to reproduce a two-class model of society. This is deeply mistaken. It has always been partly illu-sory, in that Labour has not had a strong record of winning majorities under this system. Today, however, when two-class politics is in deep disarray, all the model does is either to induce a hopeless nostalgia for a lost past, or to impose an artificially narrow discipline of two-party organisation. Once we accept that the changed electorate of the 21st century is never likely to produce the old pattern, it becomes clear that the kind of electoral system that would favour egalitarian interests is very different from one which enables an increasingly aloof party elite to keep central control and restrict the political options available to activists.

Dealing with corporate domination

However, no policies of these kinds can tackle the fundamental change which has been identified as lying behind the advance of post-democracy: the growing political power of the firm. Among earlier generations of radicals this sentence would have been the cue for proposals for the abolition of capitalism. This is no longer viable. While enthusiasm for the capitalist mode of production has recently been taken to excess (viz the cases of railways, water supply and air traffic control), no-one has yet found an effective alternative to the capitalist firm for process and product innovation and for customer responsiveness for most goods and services. The search must therefore be for ways of retaining the dynamism and enterprise of capitalism while preventing firms and their executives from exercising power to a degree incompatible with democracy. The currently fashionable reply to that proposition is that it is impossible: once we start regulating and restraining capitalist behaviour we rob it of its dynamism.

This is the bluff which the political world is afraid to call. At other times and places democracy has depended on the capacity of politicians to reduce the political power of the military while at the same time sustaining its effectiveness as a fighting force. These balances have to be found if democracy is to thrive. Such a compromise was worked out between democracy and national manufacturing capitalism in the mid-20th century. Today it is global financial capitalism which has to be brought to terms.

But to ask for this at the global level at the present time is to cry for the moon. The framework of international governance established through the World Trade Organisation, the Organisation for Economic Co-Operation and Development, the International Monetary Fund, and (for Europeans) the European Union is currently moving in the opposite direction. Virtually all measures of international economic 'reform' and liberalisation involve breaking down barriers to corporate freedom. In a paradox very familiar from capitalist economic history, although the guiding theory is the achievement of near-perfect markets, in practice trade liberalisation without regulation serves the interests of the biggest corporations, which create oligopolies rather than free markets. Most of those originate in the USA, the world's sole super-power, and can therefore add the government of that country to their lobbying strength within international organisations. And the USA is more committed to corporate freedom than most other democracies. Areas of policy previously recognised as exceptions from free trade policies, such as health or aid to poor countries are now being challenged, as in the losing struggles of the EU to protect European consumers from various chemical additives in US meat or to sustain its promises to Caribbean banana producers.

The attempt to devise policies for global economic regulation must go on, but the chances of them entering a serious inter-governmental agenda are remote.

The issue seems more manageable at a national level. The most urgent question here is reducing the overwhelming dominance that business interests have acquired within government through the various different processes identified in Section II. (Indeed, achieving this within a large number of individual states is a precondition for any international action.)

According to the neo-liberal ideology within whose terms virtually all governments today operate, these problems are resolved by establishing a proper market economy; governments and business interests got into each other's hair under the old

Keynesian and corporatist forms of social democratic economy; once free markets rule, government knows and accepts its restricted role of setting the basic legal framework; and firms, knowing that government no longer intervenes in the economy, keep out of politics. If the past 20 years have taught us anything it is the complete nonsense of this formulation. This is not only because the contracting-out of public services—a policy commended by the ideology—requires close interaction between government officials and firms. More generally and subtly, once government is seen as essentially incompetent and firms as uniquely competent as neo-liberal ideology implies, governments come under pressure to give over to firms and corporate leaders ever more control over public business. Far from clarifying the boundary between government and business, neo-liberalism has linked them in manifold new ways—but all within the former territory reserved to government.

Tackling the ensuing confusion of functions and temptations to corruption requires action at several levels. New rules are required to prevent, or at least very closely to regulate, flows of money and personnel between parties, circles of advisors and corporate lobbies. Relations between corporate donors on the one hand and public servants, public spending criteria and public policy-making on the other need to be clarified and codified. The concept of public service as a field of *sui generis* ethics and purposes needs to be re-established. It is instructive to reflect that the Victorians, archetypical capitalists as they often were, developed and enforced a profound understanding of what distinguished public service from private profit-making, without at all opposing the proper functions of the latter. The particular rules they devised may well require radical amendment in a period when understanding of how large organisations can work have advanced far beyond the model of the classic bureaucracy; but the current orthodoxy—which simply maintains that the public service has 'a lot to learn' from private business—must be improved upon.

Research is required into the lessons—both positive and negative—which are now available to us following a number of years of penetration of public services by the private sector. What is the balance of improved efficiency against distorted goals? Given that business leaders today are invited to exercise influence, through donations and sponsorship, in public areas outside the fields of their business competence, do they confront professional practice simply with commercial judgment, or with chances to display personal idiosyncrasy, and if so, what are the consequences?

The citizens' dilemma

This task of researching and rethinking the political place of firms and their leading executives is one in which many can share. But who would be the addressees of all this earnest activity? Normally of course the main answer would be organs of government, but a major theme of this pamphlet has been the way in which governmental and party policy-making machinery has itself become endogenous to the problem of the power of the corporate elite. The above call for research into the effects of the role of the private sector within public services shows this. Who is to carry out such research? Government itself is today most likely to call upon private consultancy firms to do this, itself an example of the issue in question.

In particular for Fabians, the natural addressee of policy recommendations, the Labour Party, has become part of the problem rather than the solution. True to the image of active, positive citizens which I outlined as being the lifeblood of maximalist democracy in Chapter 1, I therefore wish to end, not by elaborating the various ideas noted here for improving the quality of our democracy, but by asking what we ourselves need to do to have these issues placed on the real political agenda in the first place.

The logic of the arguments in this pamphlet seems to lead to alarmingly contradictory conclusions. On the one hand, it would seem that in post-democratic society we can no longer take for granted the commitment of particular parties to particular causes. This would lead to the conclusion that we should turn our backs on the party fight and devote our energies to cause organisations that we know will continue to press the issues about which we care. On the other hand we have also seen that the fragmentation of political action into a mass of causes and lobbies provides systematic advantages to the rich and powerful far greater than did a more party-dominated politics, where parties stood for relatively clear social constituencies. From this perspective, to desert party for cause group is only to conspire further in the triumph of post-democracy. However, again, to cling to the old model of the monolithic party is to sink into nostalgia for an irretrievable past.

Some observers connected with the New Labour search for a Third Way in politics, avoiding what they see as the cumbersome institutions of the recent past, are far more sanguine than I am at the prospect of the replacement of big party organisations by more flexible and less conventionally 'political' structures. Leading examples are Anthony Giddens in *The Third Way* (Cambridge: Polity, 1998) and Geoff Mulgan in *Politics in an Antipolitical Age* (Cambridge: Polity, 1994). However, it is striking that neither of these authors regards capitalism as problematic, or sees major blocs of corporate power as at all fundamental to the dilemmas of contemporary society.

There are ways of reconciling the contradiction between flexible new movements and solid old parties other than by pretending that problems which can be confronted only by the latter no longer exist. Party remains fundamental to the avoid-

63

ance of the anti-egalitarian tendencies of post-democracy. But we cannot rest content with working for our political goals solely by doing so through the party. We also have to work on the party from outside by assisting those causes which will sustain pressure on it. Parties which are not under pressure from causes will stay rooted in the cost world of corporate lobbying; causes which try to act without reference to building strong parties of the left will find themselves dwarfed by the corporate lobbies. We need to keep the two apparently contrasting forms of action—cause movements and parties—in relation to each other.

Mobilising new identities

However far post-democracy advances, it is unlikely that it will exhaust the capacity for new social identities to form, become aware of their outsider status in the political system, and make both noisy and articulate demands for admission, disrupting the stage-managed and sloganised world of conventional post-democratic electoral politics. We have already seen how feminist movements have provided very recent, very major instances of this. Ecological movements provide others. This constant scope for new disruptive creativity within the demos gives egalitarian democrats their main hope for the future.

Both feminist and ecological movements followed the classic pattern of past mobilisations: an identity develops and is defined by various vanguard groups. Frustrated by political exclusion, some of these become extreme and possibly violent. But if the cause has any resonance with a wider public, it spreads; its concerns filter into the language and thoughts of ordinary people who are not normally caught up in causes. It becomes incoherent and internally contradictory. The world of official politics is taken by surprise, finds the movement unmanageable and attacks it as undemocratic; more articulate demands are formulated; the elite finds means of responding to these; the movement has entered politics, and begins to experience a mixed pattern of victories and defeats.

Now, to accept this point is to invert the perspective usually adopted by the political world of what constitutes democracy and what its negation. Faced with difficult and disruptive new demands, elected politicians have one response: they themselves constitute the embodiment of democratic choice; we have our chance to make that choice in elections every few years; anyone who causes trouble in seeking major change at other times or in other ways is therefore attacking democracy itself. (Curiously, they never mention the pressures for policy favours from business interests to which they are permanently subject, but we have said enough about that.) From this perspective my creatively troublesome demos is an anti-democratic mob.

We must be careful here. At the present time, in addition to feminist and ecological movements, the groups which are seeking attention include animal rights campaigns, the Seattle and Prague global anti-capitalism campaign, the countryside lobby (including and extending into the fuel protest), racist organisations, the anti-paedophile campaign and similar incipient lynching movements. It is a terrible mistake to be gleeful every time that the political class has its feathers badly ruffled: that way lies the absurd and dangerous welcome that many have been tempted to give to Jörg Haider in Austria and his populist and racist counterparts in Belgium, Scandinavia and elsewhere. We must always discriminate, and at two levels. First is the decision whether to welcome the emergence of a particular new movement as compatible with democracy, contributing to civic vigour and preventing politics from disappearing into a manipulative game among elites. Second is the decision whether personally to support, oppose or remain indifferent to its objectives.

There is a difference in what we welcome as democrats and what we actually support as egalitarian democrats. But I would insist that it is at these points that we make our discriminations and judgments, not at the prior point on which the political class invites us to concentrate, which would have us accept as democratic only those groups and issues already fully processed by their machines. To put the point in different terms: we have to learn to distinguish between 'our' roughs and 'their' roughs. It may well be a less difficult task than distinguishing between 'our' smoothies and 'their' smoothies, which is what electoral politics requires us to do.

Loyal Labour Party members today are prone to take a hostile approach to virtually all kinds of social movement activity. During the 1980s, as described in Chapter 3, the party became embroiled in several doomed disruptive movements as its old secure bases fell apart, and it was punished heavily for it. If New Labour represents anything, it represents desperate respectability. It wants to shut the door on all unpredictable forces, old and new alike, using its advanced opinion research techniques to select, and position itself in relation to, any discontents it perceives to be emerging, keeping control, monopolising the definition of issues, *de haut en bas*. This may be necessary for a therapeutic period following the 1980s, but as a long-term strategy it involves welcoming and encouraging the entropy of political enthusiasm, and turning one's back on all new, unprocessed concerns which emerge.

The mobilising issues which will nourish the future development of the left—in particular campaigns against the consequences of uncontrolled global capitalism by the demonstrators in Seattle and Prague—are being neglected or rejected. The initiative in articulating new concerns is therefore shifting to the right —which almost by definition does not have the same fears that it might lose political respectability. If this continues, not only will the right—more specifically the Conservative Party—manage to define and orchestrate the only forms of expressed discontent to achieve political salience, but it is able falsely to represent itself as living outside the closed world of the political class.

The Labour Party itself may feel that it is still too dangerous for it to become involved in new social movements, but individuals, as well as trade unions and other organisations on the left, should see ourselves as having a continued responsibility for engagement of this kind. It is not a fact of nature that people care more about the price of petrol than they do about the stress of reconciling increasingly oppressive working hours with family life. It is possible for campaigns orchestrated by the left to be as popular as those of the right, provided the campaigns are waged. The withdrawal of genetically modified foods from supermarkets in response to consumer concern showed this. That incident left the Labour government isolated in alliance with the US chemical firms which had so successfully lobbied it through the policy-makers' ellipse, when it might have used the protests in order to fashion a popular general ecology policy.

The continuing relevance of the Labour Party

However, as noted, a return to movement politics must not imply turning our backs on party politics, which remain essential for stemming the slide into post-democratic elite domination of the political agenda, and the hopelessly one-sided odds of the politics of the lobby. Further, as I tried to show in Chapter 4, the new policy-making ellipse cannot replace all the functions of a mass membership. Parties still needs members' time and money.

As the New Labour government moves towards the end of its first term the mutual interdependence of government and party members becomes more apparent. During the fuel protests of autumn 2000 the trade unions, who had been spurned by the government, stood loyally by it, especially the Transport and General Workers Union which might well have taken a different line; while the Daily Mail constituency which the government had wooed so ardently revealed itself to be the enemy of New Labour every bit as much as it had been of Michael Foot's Labour Party of the 1980s. The emphasis of the government's policies and rhetoric began at the same time to adjust: it started to boast of its public spending on health, education and pensions rather than trying to do good by stealth as it had during the previous three years; ministers ceased vilifying school teachers and other public employees. However, at the same time it continued to ally itself with the preferences of the corporate elite; privatisation of the NHS was also initiated during the same pre-election period. The struggle for the soul of New Labour is still intense; but that is a major reason for not abandoning it.

Further, if egalitarians desert the Labour Party at the present time there is a grave risk of creating a dangerous vacuum, which might be filled in a sickening way. We have today a Labour leadership very interested in partially replacing its traditional supporters by wealthier, corporate interests. At the same time, much corporate wealth is extremely dissatisfied with the shallow, unimpressive force which the contemporary Conservative Party has become. There is a real risk that the Labour Party could actually become their preferred party. In that scenario a movement which had been constructed by the labours of ordinary working people and their sympathisers for over a century would have been hijacked by hostile interests, who had themselves trashed their own party.

Support for cause movements cannot replace the political party. However, this is not an argument for total loyalty. The more stubbornly loyal its core supporters, the more a party leadership can take them for granted and concentrate on responding to the powerful pressures being exercised upon it through the policy ellipse. In such a situation party members' strength grows as their support becomes conditional, and as this fact is made explicit and tangible. Egalitarians must therefore learn to risk a robust approach appropriate to post-democratic citizens, rewarding their party when it acts favourably and punishing it when it does not. For example, trade unions should decide annually how to allocate their political fund among a number of causes, the Labour Party being one potential candidate among them, rather than guarantee it a stream of support for a number of years.

This approach has long been practised in the USA. Although, for example, the US labour unions are strongly attached to the Democratic Party, they will be quite ruthless in backing individual Republican politicians if these are more supportive of labour's causes than the local Democrat. British politics is undergoing an Americanisation, as the political class disconnects itself from its roots in the wider society to join a self-referential world of wealthy business groups and media practitioners. In the USA there is a symmetry of infidelity between parties and their associated causes; in Britain we have loyal causes and a fickle party.

The US approach as such is possible only given the sprawling, incoherent, undisciplined character of its parties. British politics are at the other extreme of claustrophobic control, requiring loyalty at all costs for fear of helping the diametrically opposed and equally centralised opposition. The proportional representation systems of most other democracies provide something between the two. An individual or cause group has a little scope for shifting favours among different parties within the same basic political side, enabling individual parties to be rewarded or punished without hurting the side as a whole.

In the absence of proportional representation, the egalitarian British citizen is left with very little scope for autonomous political action. There is absolutely no case for considering the Conservative Party as a likely champion of renewed democracy. It is true that Conservatives now devote less time to extolling free markets and the wisdom of entrepreneurs and executives than they did in the 1980s and 1990s, or than Labour leaders do today. This is not however because they are developing a critique of contemporary capitalism, but because, unable to make a convincing move to the left, and with Labour adopting most of their economic policies, they are forced to seek out unexplored spaces on the right where Labour will not follow them. This leads them to xenophobia, an obsession with harsh punishment for offenders, and the defence of fox-hunting and the use of petrol engines. They do not even link their attempts to stir up fear of foreigners to problems of economic globalisation, as does the neo-fascist Front National in France or Pat Buchanan's ambiguous movement in the USA. Citizens concerned at the real sources of problems being posed to democracy have no need to give a second glance at current Tory populism.

The Liberal Democrats are a different matter. Partly perhaps because the two main parties have been content to leave acres of empty space to their left, partly because it has not been the target of business lobbies in the way that Labour has, the contemporary Liberal Democrats are rapidly becoming a more reliable spokesman for many of the causes typically associated with the Labour Party than the latter party itself: the strength of a universal public service within health, education, and pensions; general concern for redistribution; and issues of environmental damage. It is still reluctant to expand these themes into a criticism of global capitalism, but the question whether egalitarians or even socialists might sometimes vote Liberal Democrat rather than Labour is becoming a realistic choice in a way that has not been the case since 1918. The Green Party or, where relevant, the Scottish and Welsh Nationalists, might also appear as viable options, at least in local elections. These parties, because of their small size, have not come under pressures of the kind described in Chapter 4 and are therefore less vulnerable than Labour to being pulled towards post-democracy. At least their potential availability serves as a warning to New Labour of the risks it faces in taking its existing support base for granted.

Conclusion

So have Fabians come full circle to where Beatrice Webb started, lobbying the political elites of various parties without having one to call our own? No; because we are moving through a parabola and not a circle. We can no longer take for granted that the Labour Party is loyal to our causes; to that extent we are going out at the point where Beatrice Webb was coming in. But we have moved along the length of the parabola to a new historical point, and we carry a history of organisation-building and achievement which we must not squander. It is the duality of this situation that teaches us our apparently contradictory lessons: stay alert to the potentialities of new movements which may at first seem difficult to understand, because they may be the bearers of democracy's future vitality. Work through the lobbies of established and new cause organisations, because post-democratic politics works through lobbies. Even if the causes supported by egalitarians are always weaker there than those of the large corporations, they are weaker still if they stay out of the lobby. And work, critically and conditionally, through the party, because none of the post-democratic substitutes for it can replace its potential capacity for carrying through egalitarian policies.

Meanwhile, however, we know that on many of the major issues which currently confront us, the claims made by global firms that they will not be able to operate profitably unless free of regulation and not subordinated to criteria of welfare and redistribution will continue to trump all polite democratic debate. This was also the main burden of capitalism's political stance in the 19th and early 20th centuries. It was forced to make what in retrospect now seems to have been a temporary compromise by a complicated set of forces: its own long-term inability to secure economic stability; the unmanageable violence sometimes caused by both its own flirtations with fascism and its confrontations with communism; largely non-violent but still disruptive struggles against trade unions; the sheer inefficiency of neglected social infrastructure; the growing plausibility of social democratic parties and policy alternatives.

How essential were the reality and fears of chaos and disruption within that complex general equation? It is impossible to pretend that they played no part. Both the social compromise of the mid-20th century and the associated interlude of relatively maximal democracy, epitomes of peacefulness and order though they were in themselves, were forged in a crucible that included turmoil. It is necessary to remember that, as we condemn the anti-capitalism demonstrators in Seattle, London and Prague for their violence, their anarchism, their negative lack of viable alternatives to the capitalist economy. We must ask ourselves: without a massive escalation of truly disruptive actions of the kind that those demonstrators advocate, will anything reverse the profit calculations of global capital enough to bring its representatives to the bargaining table to accept an end to child slavery and other forms of labour degradation, to the production of levels of pollution that are now visibly destroying our atmosphere, to the wasteful use of non-renewable resources, to growing extremes of wealth and poverty both within and between nations? That is the question which most challenges the health of contemporary democracy.

References

1   It becomes increasingly difficult to know what generic term to use to identify the broad centre left. 'Socialist' is best used to define those who genuinely seek a transcendence of capitalism, which is becoming a very small category. 'Social democrat' avoids that, and identifies those who believe in using the power of democratic government and trade unions to civilise the conduct of capitalism. But there is a wider community of Liberals, Greens and others who would not subscribe fully to a social democratic agenda but who do believe in a need for a more egalitarian distribution of both wealth and power. In this pamphlet I am principally addressing fellow social democrats, but hoping to reach out also to egalitarians in the wider sense.

Paying for Progress
A New Politics of Tax for Public Spending

The Commission on Taxation and Citizenship

Taxation—and the public spending it pays for—is the subject of the fiercest political controversy. *Paying for Progress: A New Politics of Tax for Public Spending* offers a compelling new approach.

Reporting the results of new research into public attitudes towards taxation, Paying for Progress argues that the public must be 'reconnected' to the taxes they pay and the public services which these finance. To do this it proposes the greater use of 'earmarked' taxes, including a new tax to fund the National Health Service. Setting out a new philosophy of citzenship to underpin taxation policy, it recommends a series of reforms to meet the goals of social inclusion and environmental protection. And it asks: are higher taxes needed to pay for public services?

Written in a lively and accessible style for the general reader, *Paying for Progress* makes an important contribution to political thought and policy in the first decade of the 21st century. Providing key information on the UK tax system, it will also be an invaluable text for students and researchers in politics, economics, public administration, law and accountancy.

'Coherent, radical and lucid... this important book raises critical questions for the future of British politics'
Will Hutton, Chief Executive, the Industrial Society

'Highly recommended... The clarity with which it explores the facts and arguments about the tax system make it an extremely valuable text for students and researchers... it will provide a benchmark for future work on taxation reform'
Andrew Gamble, Professor of Politics, University of Sheffield

November 2000 ■ ISBN 07163 6003 9 ■ £9.95

Is the Party Over?
New Labour and the politics of participation

Paul Richards

The future does not look bright for the political party. In most of the established liberal democracies, membership levels are falling. Rapid social and technological change has undermined the relevance of traditional parties, both to politics and to people. Some have interpreted this as evidence that the party may soon be over. This pamphlet sets out an alternative vision. It argues that the mass political party—and the Labour Party specifically—can become a vibrant and viable part of civil society in the 21st century. By turning outwards towards the local community, and engaging directly with its concerns, the Party can build a dynamic base of support which is counted in millions.

March 2000 ■ ISBN 07163 0594 1 ■ £6.95

The New European Left

Edited by Gavin Kelly

With social democratic governments in power throughout most of Europe, the left of centre has a historically unique opportunity to shape a more progressive era of European politics. *The New European Left* explores the ideas, policy debates, and electoral pressures which are determining the governing agenda in four key European countries—Germany, France, Sweden and the Netherlands. The chapters are written by leading political commentators and government advisers with expert knowledge of left of centre politics in each country. A concluding chapter by Donald Sassoon, leading expert on European politics, draws out lessons for the UK from the experiences of the left of centre across Europe.

November 1999 ■ ISBN 07163 6001 2 ■ £9.95

Closing the Casino
Reform of the global financial system

John Grieve Smith

The instability of the global financial system is now a serious threat to industry and jobs throughout the world. Crises, such as those which recently beset the Asian economies, are the most extreme manifestation of this instability. Yet, exchange rate instability presents serious problems for industry world-wide. In the aftermath of the Asian crisis, there was talk of a 'new global financial architecture'. But as the threat of a wider recession has receded, Western leaders are less concerned about root and branch reform and have limited their discussions to what one American commentator called 'interior decoration' rather than 'new architecture'. Closing the Casino argues that, if governments are to reassert control over the global casino, the development of more powerful and effective machinery for international economic co-operation is the major political challenge of the coming decade. Only then will greater interdependence of national economies become a force for progress rather than a threat of disaster.

July 2000 ■ ISBN 07163 0597 6 ■ £6